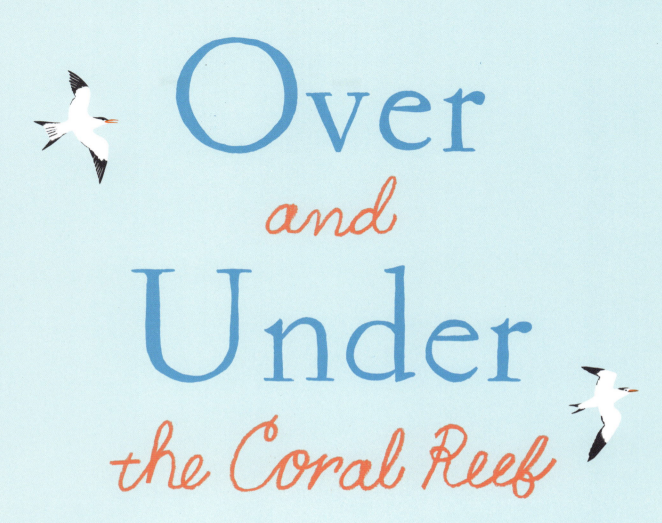

Over and Under the Coral Reef

by Kate Messner with art by Christopher Silas Neal

CHRONICLE BOOKS
SAN FRANCISCO

Over the sun-warmed sand we walk, to the edge of the sea, where waves lap the shore.

Sparkles of sunlight dance on the water.
A green sea turtle pops up her head for a
moment, then disappears into a wave.

"Where did she go?" I ask.

"Out to the reef," Papa says.

He points to a place where the
sandy seafloor darkens and royal
terns circle and call from above.

"Out on the reef there's a whole brilliant world—gardens of coral teeming with fish. Are you ready to swim with them, too?"

I wade into the waves and put on
my fins. Papa helps with my mask.

When I put my face in the water,
the sounds of the beach go silent.

All I can hear is bubbles and breath.

I spread my arms wide and float on the surface while sea stars creep over the sand.

Papa taps my shoulder and points toward deeper waters.
I kick my fins and follow him into the blue.

Below us, a stingray glides on watery wings
with a bluehead wrasse close behind.

Over the reef we float, rising and falling with the swell of the sea. Delicate sea fans sway in the current while flamingo tongue snails attach themselves to feed.

Under the reef, a moray eel lurks in his cave, waiting for prey to pass by.

Over the reef we swim, past corals in yellows and
oranges and reds, through schools of bar jacks
hunting for lunch. A banded coral shrimp shelters
in a barrel sponge, just out of sight, and an octopus
vanishes into a crack.

Up ahead, a dark shadow prowls the seafloor.
Angelfish and fairy basslets seek shelter in crevices.

I stop kicking and stare, my heart beating fast.
Papa lays a gentle hand on my shoulder and
signals that it's safe to swim on.

Slowly . . .

slowly . . .

a nurse shark circles the reef, searching the sand with a mouth made for slurping up urchins and squid.

The shark swims off, and we drift with the current. A queen conch feeds on algae in the swaying seagrass below.

Over the reef, silversides dive and turn in
unison, sparkling in the light-dappled sea.
A bigger silver something hangs in the water
nearby. Stealthy and still.

Until . . .

Whoosh!

A great barracuda darts through the school in a flash of silver scales and razor-sharp teeth.

I lift my head to find Papa.
"Did you see *that*?"

He smiles and nods as a frigate
bird soars high above.

"Come on. There's one more
spot I want to show you . . ."

We swim out to another head of coral, where black durgons and blue tangs nibble on algae and iridescent parrotfish crunch on mouthfuls of reef.

Papa points to something below us and dives.
I fill my lungs with air and follow him down
for a closer look.

Over the reef, a balloonfish floats,
all puffed up and prickly to keep
predators away.

Tucked in a crevice under the reef, two spiny
lobsters wait for the safety of night to come
out and forage for food.

We swim to the surface and take deep gulps of air.
My lips are salty as I squint into the setting sun.

"We should head back," says Papa.
But I'm not ready to go.

"Just a few minutes more?"

There's still so much to see.

Over the reef I swim, memorizing colors to keep in my mind. The dazzling blue spots of young damselfish. A rock beauty's bright yellow face. The pink-tipped tentacles of a giant anemone and the changing shades of a peacock flounder camouflaged in the sand.

And then, up ahead, a flash of black and white. A spotted eagle ray glides over the reef on graceful, magnificent wings.

I watch until it disappears into the deeper, darker blue. A tap on my shoulder tells me it's time to swim home.

Back to the beach we paddle and kick,
over seagrass where trumpet fish hide.
A creamy pink conch shell catches my
eye—now it's home for a hermit crab,
tucking in snug for the night.

We splash through the shallows and onto the beach. Sand squishes between my toes.

We hike through the mangroves toward home as the sun sinks into the sea. Curly-tailed lizards skitter over the rocks, and tree frogs call out in the dusk.

I wash the salt and sand from my skin, then sit down for supper and crawl into bed. A breeze whispers in my window, and I can still hear the waves in the dark.

I drift off to a sea song of luminous stars
and corals where octopuses hide, of slow-
swimming nurse sharks and grazing sea turtles
and stingrays that glide through the blue.

A warm ocean lullaby of color and life—and
the secret world over and under the reef.

Author's Note

When I was a little girl, I was obsessed with the ocean and thought I might like to be a marine biologist one day. While I didn't end up choosing that career path, I still love spending time in the sea, especially snorkeling on coral reefs that are teeming with life.

Coral reefs are found in tropical areas around the world—off the coasts of the Americas, Africa, Asia, and Australia. This book was inspired by the wildlife of the coral reefs in the Caribbean, where I've been lucky enough to swim with stingrays and colorful fish a number of times. When I was working on it, I spent several days snorkeling in Grand Cayman and enjoyed an especially wonderful day on the reef with John Kennedy and Kaleb Jeffers of Island Charters. I'm grateful for their knowledge and enthusiasm.

Coral reefs are actually made up of millions of tiny coral polyps. A group of corals is called a colony, and different kinds of corals create colonies with unique shapes, colors, and structures. That's how scientists identify them.

Coral reefs are not only magical to see; they're essential habitats for countless fish and other marine creatures. They also protect coastal communities from storms and erosion. Currently, coral reefs around the world are in danger due to climate change, pollution, and overfishing. Most of the work to save them will need to be done by governments passing laws to protect them. But there are some small things that everyone can do to help:

• Recycle when you can, and dispose of all garbage responsibly. Pollution (especially plastics) is harmful to reefs.

• When possible, use environmentally friendly modes of transportation, such as walking, biking, or making use of public transit. You can also save energy by turning off lights and other electronics when they're not in use. This helps to fight climate change.

• If you're lucky enough to visit a coral reef, choose sunscreen that doesn't damage corals, and be careful not to touch the reef itself. This can harm the delicate corals.

About the Animals

Many kinds of coral can make up a coral reef. Some of these include staghorn, brain coral, and elkhorn.

Staghorn corals (*Acropora cervicornis*) prefer calmer reef areas with clear water. This is the fastest-growing coral species in the western Atlantic, and colonies can reach 4 feet (1.2 metres) tall and 6 feet (1.8 metres) in diameter.

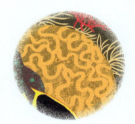

Common brain corals (*Diploria strigosa*) form round underwater heads that can grow to be up to 6 feet (1.8 metres) in diameter. Some of the largest brain corals are hundreds of years old.

Elkhorn corals (*Acropora palmata*) prefer habitats with strong currents and plenty of waves. Elkhorn coral polyps feed at night, but they can also photosynthesize and make food from sunlight during the day.

Green sea turtles (*Chelonia mydas*) are often seen swimming over coral reefs or grazing on seagrass. They can live for up to 75 years and grow to be up to 4 feet (1.2 metres) long. Some migrate over 1,000 miles (1,610 kilometres) to reach the beaches where they hatched, now to nest. Green sea turtles are endangered due to overharvesting of both adults and eggs. They're also threatened by plastic litter, which they often mistake for food.

Royal terns (*Thalasseus maximus*) are common Caribbean birds that often breed in colonies on islands, laying their eggs in the sand. They're frequently seen around coral reefs, hovering and diving into the waves for small fish.

Red cushion sea stars (*Oreaster reticulatus*) can grow to be up to 20 inches (50.8 centimetres). Their diet includes algae, sponges, and invertebrates. Sea stars have a unique way of eating. As they move over sand, they send stomach tissue out from their bodies to digest whatever food is there. Then they suck their stomachs back in and continue on their way.

Southern stingrays (*Dasyatis americana*) can grow to have a wingspan of over 6 feet (1.8 metres). They feed by flapping their wings to uncover mollusks and crustaceans in the sand and then sucking the creatures into their mouths. Stingrays aren't aggressive, but they do have venomous barbs at the bases of their tails, which they use for self-defense.

Bluehead wrasses (*Thalassoma bifasciatum*) grow to be up to 10 inches (25.4 centimetres) long. They start life as females but can change sex, and some become males later on. (That's when their heads turn blue.) Bluehead wrasses may act as cleaner fish for larger fish, nibbling parasites off their skin.

Common sea fans (*Gorgonia ventalina*) are actually colonies of coral polyps held together by their external skeletons. They're usually purple but can also be yellow or brown, and they can grow to be up to 6 feet (1.8 metres) tall. They feed by filtering zooplankton from water currents.

Flamingo tongue snails (*Cyphoma gibbous*) are small, brightly colored marine snails that grow to be about 1 inch (2.5 centimetres) long. They feed on sea fans and other gorgonians, or soft corals. The flesh of these corals contains toxic chemicals, but flamingo tongue snails have adapted to be able to eat them, incorporating the chemicals into their own flesh to help keep predators away.

Green moray eels (*Gymnothorax funebris*) can grow to be over 6 feet (1.8 metres) long but are usually about half that size. They're solitary fish that spend their days hiding in cracks and crevices, most often feeding at night. They don't see very well, so they use their sense of smell to hunt.

Bar jacks (*Caranx ruber*) can grow to be over 2 feet (0.6 metres) long. They usually school near coral reefs, feeding on shrimp and other invertebrates. Sometimes they like to follow stingrays, which often scare up prey from under the sand.

Banded coral shrimp (*Stenopus hispidus*) frequently grow to be 2–3 inches (5.1–7.6 centimetres) long. They hide from predators in sponges and reef crevices and often pair up to defend their territories. Coral shrimp eat small fish, other crustaceans, snails, and worms.

Giant barrel sponges (*Xestospongia muta*) are sometimes called the redwoods of the coral reef because of their size and life expectancy. They can grow to be well over 3 feet (0.9 metres) tall and 6 feet (1.8 metres) across, and they may live for 2,000 years. They feed by drawing in water through their walls, filtering the food particles, and then expelling the water through openings at their tops.

Caribbean reef octopuses (*Octopus briareus*) can grow to be about 2 feet (0.6 metres) long with their arms spread out. They're able to change color, texture, and shape for camouflage. Octopuses most often hide in caves and crevices during the day and come out at night to hunt for clams, crustaceans, snails, and small fish.

French angelfish (*Pomacanthus paru*) typically grow to be about 16 inches (40.6 centimetres) long. Juveniles sometimes act as cleaner fish, eating parasites off other fish, while adults most often feed on sponges and algae. Their predators include large groupers and sharks. When those fish show up to hunt, angelfish often take cover in reef cracks and crevices.

Fairy basslets (*Gramma loreto*) are tiny fish that top out at about 3 inches (7.6 centimetres) long. They love reef walls that are full of caves and ledges for hiding. They eat floating plankton, crustaceans, and sometimes parasites from other fish. Fairy basslets often hide at night, when snappers, groupers, and moray eels are hunting.

Nurse sharks (*Ginglymostoma cirratum*) can grow to be over 9 feet (2.7 metres) long. Their jaws are specially designed for crunching on conchs, lobsters, and crabs. Nurse sharks hunt mostly at night and can be found resting in caves and under coral ledges during the day. Their mouths have whisker-like barbels that help them search for prey to slurp up from the sand.

Queen conchs (*Strombus gigas*) are the largest marine snails in the world. They can grow to up to 12 inches (30.5 centimetres) and may live for up to 30 years. Frequently seen in sandy reef areas, they eat algae and decomposing seagrass. When predators such as sharks and rays are on the prowl, queen conchs retreat into their shells for protection.

Reef silversides (*Hypoatherina harringtonensis*) are tiny schooling fish commonly found around coral reefs. They grow to be just up to 4 inches (10.2 centimetres) long and swim in tightly packed schools for protection from predators.

Great barracudas (*Sphyraena barracuda*) can grow to be 6 feet (1.8 metres) long and over 100 pounds (45.4 kilograms). They feed on many kinds of fish, including jacks, grunts, groupers, snappers, and even other barracudas. They have keen eyesight and are among the fastest fish in the sea, reaching speeds over 30 miles (48.3 kilometres) per hour.

Magnificent frigate birds (*Fregata magnificens*) are easily identified by their long, forked tails. They often soar high above the sea and look as if they're floating in the sky. They don't land in the water or dive; instead, they hunt by scooping fish from the water's surface or by chasing and harassing other seabirds, forcing them to drop or regurgitate prey that the frigate birds then snatch out of midair. Males have bright red throat pouches that they inflate when they're courting mates.

Black durgons (*Melichthys niger*) can be up to 20 inches (50.8 centimetres) long and may swim in schools of a couple hundred fish. They eat reef algae, as well as plant and animal plankton drifting in the water. Their predators include large groupers, moray eels, snappers, and barracudas.

Blue tangs (*Acanthurus coeruleus*) can grow to be over 1 foot (0.3 metres) long. They sometimes school with other fish, grazing on algae during the day and hiding in cracks and crevices at night.

Stoplight parrotfish (*Sparisoma viride*) become more colorful and can change sex from female to male as they get older. Parrotfish bite off pieces of reef and chew them up to eat the plants, algae, and other small organisms that live on the coral. Then they spit out the rest.

Balloonfish (*Diodon holocanthus*), or spiny porcupine fish, can grow to be 1.5 feet (0.5 metres) long. They're slow swimmers, so they have other ways to avoid becoming prey for bigger fish. When threatened or alarmed, balloonfish can inflate their bodies to up to twice their normal size, so their spines stick out to scare off predators.

Caribbean spiny lobsters (*Panulirus argus*) spend their days hiding in caves and crevices, coming out at night to search for snails, crabs, clams, and dead and decaying creatures to eat. These lobsters migrate each fall, marching single file into deeper waters where they'll spend the winter.

Yellowtail damselfish (*Microspathodon chrysurus*) grow to be about 8 inches (20.3 centimetres) long and are commonly seen swimming among the branches of staghorn coral. They're defensive of their territories—the algae gardens where they eat. When young, they're black with bright blue spots.

Rock beauties (*Holacanthus tricolor*) are the smallest angelfish in the Atlantic and can grow to be almost 10 inches (25 centimetres) long. They eat sponges and sometimes corals and algae. Rock beauties are prey for a number of larger fish, including snappers.

Giant anemones (*Condylactis gigantea*) can live for over 75 years if they can avoid being eaten. They come in many colors and often have pink- or purple-tipped tentacles that sting and paralyze prey. Giant anemones eat small fish, shrimp, and worms. They're most often seen attached to coral reefs but are also able to crawl.

 **Peacock flounders** (*Bothus lunatus*) are most often spotted partially buried in sand near coral reefs and seagrass. They feed on small fish, crustaceans, and small octopuses. They're able to change color for camouflage when threatened by predators, such as sharks and groupers.

 **Spotted eagle rays** (*Aetobatus narinari*) can be up to 16 feet (4.9 metres) long, with a wingspan of 10 feet (3 metres). They eat conchs, lobsters, clams, and crabs. Electroreceptors in their snouts help them search for prey buried in the sand.

 **Atlantic trumpet fish** (*Aulostomus maculatus*) can grow to be 3 feet (0.9 metres) long. They can swim vertically or horizontally and use camouflage to conceal themselves in soft corals and seagrass. They eat crustaceans and small fish, often hunting by ambush—hiding in the coral until it's time to strike.

 **Giant hermit crabs** (*Petrochirus diogenes*) have hairy red bodies and large claws and are frequently found in conch shells. They often eat algae and small invertebrates, but sometimes they attack and eat a conch, then take over its shell.

 **Curly-tailed lizards** (*Leiocephalus carinatus*), or saw-scaled curlytails, can grow to be over 5 inches (12.7 centimetres) long, not including their tails. Often found around coastal beaches and scrublands, males curl their tails to deter predators.

 **Cuban tree frogs** (*Osteopilus septentrionalis*) are the largest tree frogs in the Caribbean and North America. They eat insects, frogs, lizards, and other small animals. Their calls, which sound like raspy snores, are frequently heard on Caribbean islands.

Further Reading

You can explore the following books and websites to learn more about coral reefs:

Books:

The Brilliant Deep: Rebuilding the World's Coral Reefs by Kate Messner and Matthew Forsythe. Chronicle Books, 2018.

Coral Reefs: A Journey through an Aquatic World Full of Wonder by Jason Chin. Flash Point, 2011.

Coral Reefs: Cities of the Ocean (Science Comics) by Maris Wicks. First Second, 2016.

Where Is the Great Barrier Reef? by Nico Medina and John Hinderliter. Grosset and Dunlap, 2016.

Websites:

Aquarium of the Pacific. Coral Reefs: Nature's Underwater Cities.

      www.aquariumofpacific.org/exhibits/coralreefs

Coral Reef Alliance. Kids' Guide to Coral Reef Conservation.

      coral.org/en/blog/kids-guide-to-coral-reef-conservation/

Monterey Bay Aquarium. Coral Reefs.

      www.montereybayaquarium.org/animals/habitats/coral-reefs

National Oceanic and Atmospheric Administration. Why Are Coral Reefs Important?

      oceanservice.noaa.gov/education/tutorial_corals/coral07_importance.html

Smithsonian Ocean Portal. Corals and Coral Reefs.

      ocean.si.edu/ocean-life/invertebrates/corals-and-coral-reefs

For Beau —K. M.

For Jasper and River —C. S. N.

Library of Congress Cataloging-in-Publication Data available.

ISBN 978-1-7972-2535-7

Manufactured in China.

Design by Sandy Frank.
Typeset in Jannon Antiqua.
The illustrations in this book were rendered in mixed media.

10 9 8 7 6 5 4 3 2 1

Chronicle books and gifts are available at special quantity discounts
to corporations, professional associations, literacy programs, and other
organizations. For details and discount information, please contact our
premiums department at corporategifts@chroniclebooks.com or at
1-800-759-0190.

Chronicle Books LLC
680 Second Street
San Francisco, California 94107

Chronicle Books—we see things differently.
Become part of our community at www.chroniclekids.com.